MASTERING

the Flute

with

William Bennett

MASTERING
the *Flute*
with
William Bennett

Roderick Seed

Foreword by

WILLIAM BENNETT

INDIANA UNIVERSITY PRESS

This book is a publication of

INDIANA UNIVERSITY PRESS
Office of Scholarly Publishing
Herman B Wells Library 350
1320 East 10th Street
Bloomington, Indiana 47405 USA
iupress.indiana.edu

The paper used in this publication meets the minimum requirements of the
American National Standard for Information Sciences—Permanence of Paper
for Printed Library Materials, ANSI Z39.48-1992.

Manufactured in the United States of America

Library of Congress Cataloging-in-Publication Data

Names: Seed, Roderick, author.
Title: Mastering the flute with William Bennett / Roderick Seed ; foreword by
    William Bennett.
Description: Bloomington : Indiana University Press, 2018. | Includes
    bibliographical references and index.
Identifiers: LCCN 2017027711 (print) | LCCN 2017030067 (ebook) | ISBN
    9780253031648 (e-book) | ISBN 9780253031631 (pbk. : alk. paper)
Subjects: LCSH: Flute—Methods. | Flute—Instruction and study. | Bennett,
    William, 1936-
Classification: LCC MT340 (ebook) | LCC MT340 .S44 2018 (print) | DDC
    788.3/2193—dc23
LC record available at https://lccn.loc.gov/2017027711

1 2 3 4 5 23 22 21 20 19 18

Dedicated to Sebastian Bell,
a great flute player, mentor, and friend

Contents

Foreword

I AM VERY PLEASED to introduce this book written by Roderick Seed, whom I had the pleasure of teaching at the Royal Academy of Music in London and in my International Flute Summer School.

The exercises that Roderick has compiled and explained are inspired from my own studies with teachers such as Geoffrey Gilbert and Marcel Moyse and years of self-discovery. One of the most important lessons from Marcel Moyse was finding a reaction in the tone and how this could make the flute as expressive as other dignified instruments, such as the violin or the human voice. Finding a sound that is colorful, expressive, and resonant was inspired by listening to the great French players like Fernand Dufrène and Marcel Moyse and singers like Janet Baker.

Roderick has collected a wide range of exercises covering many topics that give the flute player the tools to play with different dynamics and a range of expression, and simultaneously helping them with associated technical difficulties such as pitch control.

Roderick has introduced my approach to the flute in a clear and logical way with his own insights and experiences. I am happy to have this all written down so eloquently by Roderick and I hope the reader finds this book to be useful in their own exploration of how to make the flute an instrument of dignity and expression.

William Bennett, 2016

Acknowledgments

I AM VERY GRATEFUL for the support and encouragement given by William and Michie Bennett. I am constantly inspired by their dedication to making the flute a dignified, expressive instrument and their generosity in passing on their knowledge to generations of flute players.

Thank you to my friends and family who have all been so supportive and helpful.

Many thanks to all my teachers over the years for their wisdom and support.

MASTERING
the Flute
with
William Bennett

Introduction

WILLIAM BENNETT ("WIBB"), OBE, is one of the most inspirational figures in flute playing today, having taught and performed all over the world at the highest level for over fifty years. His past students can be seen in the world's most prestigious orchestras and performing as soloists in their own right.

One cannot help but be moved by William Bennett's musicianship and beautiful, colorful sound. Flute players who have studied with him share many common ideals of intonation, phrasing, and sound while retaining their own self-expression so that each student sounds different—a truly remarkable testament to Bennett's unique teaching style. Students flock from all over the world to attend his annual summer school.

When I first started learning the flute, my father bought a cassette tape of flute concerti recorded by various artists that we listened to in the car after school. My favorites were all the ones played by William Bennett! I was fifteen years old when I first attended Wibb's master class at the Royal Academy of Music and was so entranced by his teaching and huge, colorful sound that I went to his summer school every year until the age of twenty-two, after which I attended as a Teaching Assistant in 2009 and 2010. I also studied with him at the Royal Academy of Music in London. Having given lessons and classes myself, I felt the need to put down on paper the principles of Wibb's method with some useful exercises for daily practice, so that flute players could understand it in more detail. These exercises are the backbone to my daily routine, and I teach them to my own students. I wrote some of the exercises myself, while others are reproduced here with William Bennett's kind permission.

This book contains topics that William Bennett teaches all his students, but it does not contain everything he ever said. The aim of this book is to introduce some exercises to students wishing to take their flute playing to the next level. It will also help deepen the reader's knowledge and enjoyment of flute playing and perhaps give an interesting insight to Wibb's approach as a flute player and musician.

ONE

Finding a Sound

FLUTES ARE OFTEN known for being easy instruments to start on. Many people can find a sound of some sort by simply blowing across the embouchure hole, much like blowing across an empty water bottle. But how does it work?

A sound is made when air is blown across the mouth hole. There is then a fluctuation of the airstream above and below the outer edge. Some air goes below the outer edge and travels into the bore of the flute, setting up a series of oscillations down the instrument, which then leads to a sound being created.

Finding Where the Note Speaks

To practice finding a sound, we can find where the flute "speaks," or the point where air becomes sound. To do this, we need to train our lips to be flexible. Let's start without the flute:

Blow on your hand and imagine *gently* blowing out a single candle (not ten!). To blow out a candle, our airstream needs to be focused and well directed.

Is the column of air focused or does it spread out? It should be focused. Air that is too spread out will result in an unfocused sound. Aim the airstream to the middle of your hand.

Now, can you move the airstream up and down by using your lower lip or jaw? Bring the lower lip forward to move the airstream up and bring the lower lip back to move the airstream down. Allow your jaw to move slightly in accordance with the lower lip. To help, you can think of the words "oo" (jaw forward) and "ah" (jaw back). Feel the air move gradually up and down. Is the air moving steadily or is it shaky? Try to keep it steady.

Focus on blowing gently up and down. Resist the urge to bring your lips into a smile. Have a look in the mirror and watch your lower lip. Try not to move your head up and down while doing this.

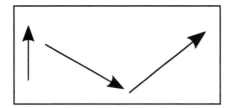

Your lips should be round and the air should have a clear direction. Try doing the same movement with your lips, but squeezed into a smile. Compare how little the air can move up and down when your lips are tight with how far it can move when your lips do not have this undue tension.

Now try the same with the flute. Finger the note C2. Start by blowing above the embouchure hole so that all you can hear is air (no sound). **Slowly** bring the airstream down like you did on your hand and listen carefully.

EXAMPLE 1.1. Finding where the note speaks.

Follow these steps, referring to the points in example 1.1:

Blow up so there is no sound and slowly bring the airstream down until air becomes sound.

This is the point where the note speaks.

Blow up again from point b until there is no sound again.

Where does the sound begin? When you find that point, start again and repeat the process. Once you have found that point many times, try to reduce the time it takes to find it by starting from a position closer to the speaking point. However, make sure you start from point a each time (where there is no sound). The more you practice this, the closer point a will get to point b. This is training for your lip muscles and the basis for "soft attack," which we will look at in chapter 4.

Messa di voce **exercise**

Try to play from the speaking point of the note and hold it for 8 beats. You can increase the volume of sound slightly so that you are blowing freely. Then allow the sound to fade again. This is what many singers and string players practice—it's called *messa di voce* ("placing of voice"). Try example 1.2 below. Once you are comfortable with the low notes at the beginning, apply the same approach to the harmonics, remembering to keep the fingering the same. Take your time and repeat where necessary. Breathe between each note so that you practice the process of beginning the note from above each time. Try to keep the dynamic within the range of *pianissimo* to *mezzo piano*.

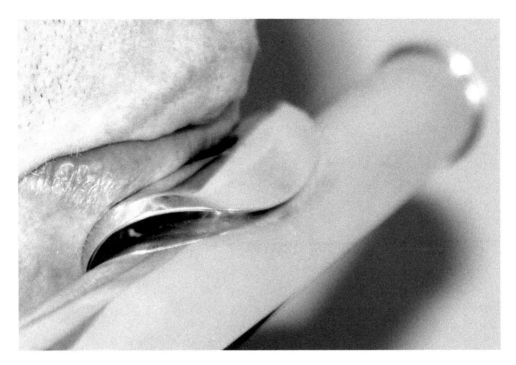

FIGURE I.2. Finding where the note speaks.

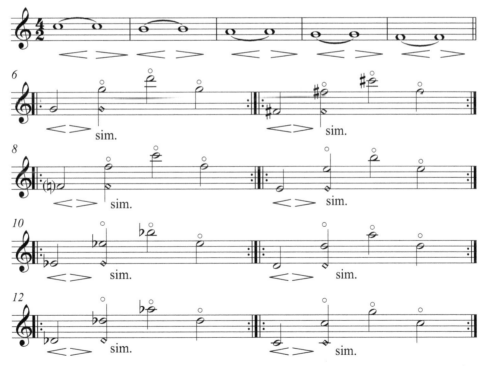

EXAMPLE I.2. *Messa di voce* exercise.

TWO

Harmonics in Tune Tone

ONCE YOU HAVE found a sound, the next step is to develop it so that it can be resonant and vibrant.

To get a large, full sound, we do not actually need to use a lot of air. This is a common misconception. When the harmonics are in tune, the sound will ring and project to the back of any concert hall, even in a soft dynamic. Many people blow too hard in order to get a big sound, but this is not an efficient way of producing a full enveloping sound.

Harmonics in Tune

So, what does it mean when we say *harmonics in tune*?

Every note on every instrument has its own harmonic series, made up of the fundamental (the note that is played) and the overtones. On flutes, the basic harmonic series for low C (for example) is as follows:

EXAMPLE 2.1. The harmonic series for the note C.

To find a *harmonics in tune* tone, we need to make sure all of the harmonics are in their right place. Practically speaking, we can only check the second and third harmonics (the octave and the 5th above that).

Position of the Headjoint

First, the position of the headjoint (how far it is pulled out) needs to be considered. Each flute has its own *in-tune position*, depending on its make and scale. Some flutes are pitched at A = 440 Hz while others may be A = 442 Hz or A = 444 Hz. The *in-tune position* can be found by doing this simple exercise:

First, tune the octave.

EXAMPLE 2.2. Exercise for tuning the octave to find an in-tune position.

It is necessary for the column of air to double in speed to make the note go up the octave from C1 to C2, but try to achieve this by slightly raising the jet of air with a very subtle pressure change in the lips (don't simply blow twice as hard!). When you have managed to get the C2 this way, then change your fingers to make the real fingering for C2. Listen carefully to the pitch. How does it compare with the pitch of the harmonic fingering? It should be the same. If the real note is **flatter** than the harmonic, then **push in** the headjoint. If the real note is **sharper** than the harmonic, **pull out** the headjoint. Don't be tempted to adjust with your lips after hearing a difference in pitch.

Next, tune the 5th above the octave. Always start from the bottom and work your way up to the next harmonic without force. Please note that the third harmonic, because it is a 12th above the fundamental (compound perfect 5th), should be a very small degree sharper than the real fingering. Your goal is to make sure that the harmonic is only *slightly* sharper than the real fingering. Please see chapter 8 on intonation.

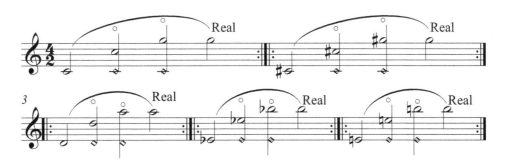

EXAMPLE 2.3. Exercise for tuning the next harmonic to find an in-tune position.

Again, using example 2.3, compare the pitches of the harmonic and real fingerings of all the notes. Make note of any notes that are out of place. The position of your headjoint where the real fingering pitches match the harmonic pitches is your *in-tune position*. You will need to adjust this position when tuning to other instruments for various reasons (temperature, body condition, pitch of the other instruments, etc.). If you are to play with a piano, warm your flute well and then play your A with a good tone (the sound you will play your piece with) before comparing it with the A on the piano. This will mean that you are comparing the difference between your possibly different As. Whereas, if you let the piano play the A first, it is likely that you will use your lips to adjust to the pitch of the piano, and this will probably mean that you will compromise the quality of your tone by sharpening or flattening everything.

Please note that moving the headjoint in or out affects the notes played by your left hand (C–G♯) *more than* the notes in your right hand (G–D), so we need to be flexible with our lips to fine-tune our instrument. Pulling out the footjoint can help if D2 is sharp. We will look more at intonation in chapter 8.

To find a *harmonics in tune* tone, we need to make sure that the harmonics present in the fundamental's sound (the overtones) are in tune. For this, we use pitch bending (or note bending).

Pitch Bending

In the first chapter, we looked at directing the air up and down using our lower lip to find the beginning of a note. We can purposefully change the pitch of a note by covering and uncovering the embouchure hole of the flute with our lower lip. Finger a C2 and start by blowing up, then gradually lower the airstream, covering the embouchure hole more and more, making the pitch flatter and flatter. Then from that covered position, raise the airstream back up to a sounding C2. Remember to keep your lips free of undue tension. See how flat and sharp you can make the note. William Bennett can flatten up to a minor 3rd on most notes in the low register, and very occasionally to a major 3rd (although this is virtually inaudible as the mouth hole must be almost completely covered).

Finger one note for this exercise. The pitches above are approximate and will vary depending on how much you can bend the note. You can do this exercise on any note, but C2 is considered the most flexible one to start with.

Finger C natural, blow above the mouth hole and gradually bring the air stream down

Flatten the note as far as you can manage and then gradually bring the airstream back up to your best sounding C natural

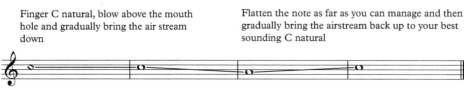

EXAMPLE 2.4. Pitch-bending exercise.

Points to consider:

- Don't roll the flute in and out with your hands. This can change the pitch, but if you need to make pitch adjustments in a passage of music, you don't want to be rolling your flute all the time and causing undue tension in your body, or losing tonal stability.

- Don't move your head up and down. Again, this changes the pitch, but doing this too often will cause tension in your neck and cause your sound to constrict. A little movement is fine, but to make big or quick pitch changes, this method is not suitable.

- **DO** use your lower lip and jaw to control the pitch, and work every day to get a bit further than you did the previous day. Check your movement in the mirror.

FIGURE 2.1. Covering the mouth hole by bringing the lower lip and jaw back to flatten the pitch.

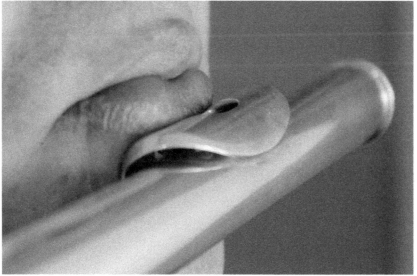

FIGURE 2.2. Uncovering the mouth hole by bringing the jaw and lower lip forward to raise the pitch.

Your *harmonics in tune* tone is the one that is somewhere in the middle of being too uncovered and too covered. Without blowing more, it will sound larger and have a natural resonance. A very uncovered (sharp) sound will produce a *flat* octave (first harmonic), that is, the octave will be too narrow. A very covered (flat) sound will produce a *sharp* octave, that is, the octave will be too wide. Therefore, practice the exercise below (ex. 2.5) slowly, listening very carefully to the distance between your fundamental and the first harmonic/octave.

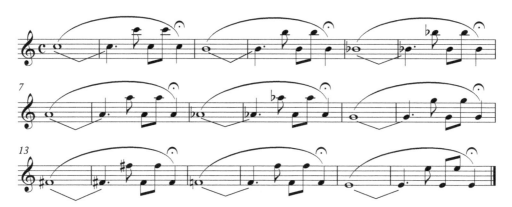

EXAMPLE 2.5. Exercise for checking the octave after pitch bending.

Checking the Octave

Remember to finger one note at a time and bend it with your lower lip. Repeat until you find the true octave and end on a sustained note that sounds rich and full. Air has three basic components: direction, volume, and speed, which we will discuss in chapter 3. To play an octave higher, the air speed needs to **double**, and the airstream is raised with the lower lip, but the *volume of the air remains constant.* In other words, don't simply blow more to get a note an octave higher.

This is your in-tune sound, so remember it! This is a good exercise to do before starting scales, so that you can spread your good *harmonics in tune* sound through all the notes.

I learned the following exercise with Wibb. It is a variation of a vocalise he learned from Geoffrey Gilbert for keeping the sound even and checking the intonation of the octave. Make sure you start with a good sound before moving to the next note.

EXAMPLE 2.6. Vocalise for an even sound.

Here is a variation of the above exercise, where you transfer your best sound to the next sequence. Use the pick-ups at the end of each bar to pull your sound through to an even better note. Start by checking the harmonic C and the real fingering. If you notice that the sound changes (loses focus or color), go back one sequence where it sounded better and continue from there.

EXAMPLE 2.7. Variation for sustaining the color to low C.

Be careful of the rhythm—it is in $\frac{6}{4}$ (not $\frac{3}{2}$ or $\frac{12}{8}$). In other words, place the stress on the first beat and then on the fourth beat of each bar, using the third and fifth beats as pick-ups. After showing the correct stress, aim for a sustained legato line.

EXAMPLE 2.8. Incorrect and correct stress.

You can do the same exercise going up. Keep going until you reach the highest C.

EXAMPLE 2.9. Sustain the color to top C.

THREE

Reaction in the Sound

"When I do something in my body, the flute—it reacts!"

Marcel Moyse

WILLIAM BENNETT'S LESSONS with the legendary Marcel Moyse influenced his playing and teaching considerably. To paraphrase the quote above: when we do something inside our bodies, the flute reacts, just as when a singer sings "ha-ha-ha-ha" or when a piano key's hammer hits a string. There is an initial attack, followed by a decay. It could be illustrated like this:

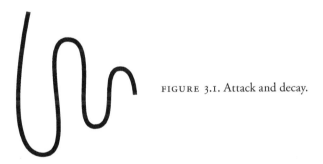

FIGURE 3.1. Attack and decay.

This can be simplified to the shape in figure 3.2. Notice how the beginning of the note is not square, but rounded. If you sing any note with the word "hah," you will notice that the air moves over the vocal chords just before the note speaks. This avoids a harsh, explosive beginning, and produces rather a warm full sound. We will look at different attacks in chapter 4.

FIGURE 3.2. Simplified shape for attack and decay.

One should start with a fairly strong beginning to the note which should then diminish, like a church bell (see "Bell Tones" below). If we simply blow hard for the beginning of the note and gradually blow less as the note diminishes we will hear an unpleasant drop in pitch. Using the technique we learned earlier in "Pitch Bending," we need to lower the jet of air and cover the embouchure hole for the louder start of the note (to prevent it becoming too sharp) and to gradually lift the jet of air as the notes becomes softer (to prevent it from becoming flat as it diminishes). This can be achieved by a simple yet subtle movement of the lips and jaw. Try singing "dao" or "daaawoooo," where the lips and jaw come forward to say the "ooo" sound for the end of the note. Then try example 3.1, first listening to how the pitch changes when you don't adjust with the lower lip. After that, try to keep the pitch even.

EXAMPLE 3.1. Exercise for attack and decay on a single note.

Getting the Flute to React

Without adjusting the pitch (don't move your lower lip), practice the *Allemande* from J. S. Bach's Partita in A Minor without the tongue, at a slow tempo, focusing on getting a good attack and decay on each note (think "ha ha ha"). Allow the air to bounce and let the flute respond to it. You can also practice this by breathing in between each note, much like a dog panting.

EXAMPLE 3.2. J. S. Bach, "Allemande" from Partita in A minor for Flute, BWV 1013, mm. 1–4.

Vibrato Exercise

This is an exercise to help feel what happens in our bodies when we use vibrato. Vibrato is a fluctuation of pitch which can be observed in watching string players, but on the flute or voice it is caused by pressure changes in the blowing mechanism. We want to hear the pitch change. Therefore, without moving the lower lip, blow more and allow the pitch to rise. As the sound decays, the pitch drops. Try to move the pitch up and down as in figure 3.3 by blowing more and then less.

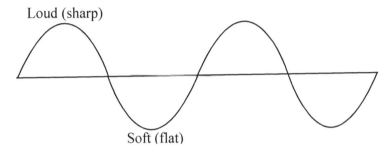

FIGURE 3.3. Vibrato—a fluctuation of pitch.

Hold one note and pulse the rhythms in example 3.3 with your abdominal muscles to make a vibrato that speeds up and slows down. Practice it first with a deep, wide vibrato and then a shallow vibrato. For a deep vibrato, more pitch variation is required, so a greater effort is required from the abdominal muscles. This is also a good exercise for filling out your sound. Allow the pitch to fluctuate without adjusting the lips. Repeat each bar as indicated. Remember, don't use the tongue.

EXAMPLE 3.3. Vibrato exercise.

After you have played this, just hold the note you were playing *without trying* to vibrate and you will notice that the sound is already more alive.

"Cardiogram" Exercise

This is another exercise for getting a reaction in the sound. As in the cardiogram in figure 3.4, play a long note with a good tone and give it sudden thrusts of air so that the octave sounds. Always come back to a good, in-tune fundamental. See if you can get the other harmonics out—these will require more effort. You can do this on any note.

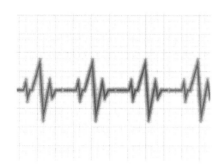

FIGURE 3.4. An example of an electrocardiogram.

EXAMPLE 3.4 Electrocardiogram exercise.

Bell Tones

EXAMPLE 3.5. S. Karg-Elert, *Chaconne* from *30 Caprices for Flute Solo*, op. 107, no. 30, mm. 1–4.

Try getting a good attack and decay on the four notes above, as if they were being struck on four different bells. This time, try to keep the pitch constant and make sure the sound remains focused. Look at figure 3.6 below to guide you. Uncovering too much will give the note an airy quality. Remember not to roll the flute with your hands—try to use only the lower lip or jaw.

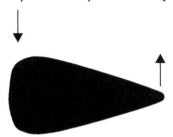

FIGURE 3.6. Every attack and decay requires the flute player to cover and gradually uncover with the lower lip.

forte **piano**

Cover the mouth hole with the lower lip, then lift the airstream by gradually *uncovering* it with the lower lip.

With a diminuendo on a single note, the volume of air reduces toward the end of the note, but the *air speed should remain constant.* The direction of the air will need to be raised to avoid the pitch falling. If the air speed drops, the sound will lose its quality.

Now try the Bach *Allemande* again, but this time *in tune,* by making the appropriate adjustment with your lower lip and jaw.

The Three Components of Air

Practice each of the three components:

- air speed,
- air direction, and
- volume (amount) of air

by isolating them in the following exercise. Try to go from one harmonic to the next smoothly without changing the dynamic. To go from a low note to a higher note, the air speed needs to increase and the direction of the air needs to be raised. For the dynamic to stay the same, the volume or amount of air should stay the same. Air speed is raised by a combination of bringing the lips together (creating a smaller aperture) and using a slight abdominal pressure. Try blowing on your hand (as we did in chap. 1) and feel the difference between fast and slow air. Look in a mirror to observe your embouchure as you do this.

It is important to distinguish the difference between the amount of air we use and the speed at which it travels across the flute. One can take the example of water running out of a hose. When you turn on a tap, water runs freely out of the opening of the hose at a constant rate. If you partially cover the opening of the hose with your thumb, (decreasing the size of the hole) you will notice that the water comes out faster, like a spray. The same amount of water is being released, but it is being forced through a smaller area, causing an increase in the speed at which it escapes. The same principle applies to flute playing, but instead of water, we have air. Our lips and the size of the hole between them when we blow is represented by the opening of the hose. Decreasing the size of the hole between our lips by bringing them closer together makes the air come out faster, without using more air by blowing harder.

When you can do the whole exercise in a comfortable *mf,* practice it in another dynamic, thereby changing the *volume* of air to get a different dynamic. Be careful not to overblow and distort the sound. For louder dynamics, blow with a bit more abdominal pressure, but take care to lower the airstream so the intonation remains pure. For softer dynamics, blow more gently and raise the airstream. Keep the space inside the mouth and throat open, so that the sound does not tighten.

EXAMPLE 3.6. Exercise for changing the air speed and direction.

To make this a harder exercise, practice playing a diminuendo on each note (within the prescribed dynamic), so you are combining all the properties of air:

- Speed (faster for the higher notes)
- Volume (more at the beginning of each note)
- Direction (cover and uncover by lowering and lifting the airstream)

EXAMPLE 3.7. Exercise for combining all components of air.

Different Lengths of Notes

No matter what length the note is, we need to do the cover/uncover movement with our lips to counter any change in pitch. Therefore, practice decays of different lengths.

Try the exercise below. On a B2, play each note *forte* and diminish to *pianissimo*.

EXAMPLE 3.8. Exercise for attack and decay on notes of different lengths.

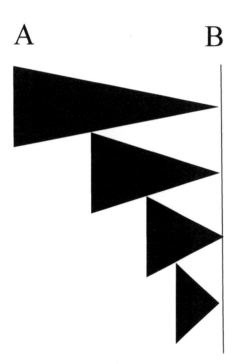

FIGURE 3.7. Attack and decay on notes of different lengths .

One way to visualize this exercise is to walk from one point of the room to another while playing a controlled diminuendo. At point A, I always play *forte* and by point B I have done a diminuendo to *pianissimo*.

By reducing the distance between A and B, but still having to do the same level of diminuendo (*forte* to *pianissimo*), we simply need to adjust with our lips more quickly. By always finishing at the same place (point B), we have a destination where the sound should always reach the same dynamic level. Then try the exercise without walking, but keeping the visual in mind.

Doing the same operation but in reverse is also very useful, that is, playing a crescendo from nothing, but at different rates. If you are doing this, don't finish the note suddenly—take care that it still sounds beautiful. This is an extension of the *messa di voce* exercise (see ex. 1.2).

Different Note Shapes

Here are some examples of different note shapes.

Martellato sostenuto

Sustain the sound and color—uncover just toward the end of the note to help with rearticulation.

FIGURE 3.8. *Martellato sostenuto* shape.

Sfz (sforzando) or fp

This requires a quick adjustment so we hear a sudden drop in dynamic, but sustain the note in *piano* for its full value.

FIGURE 3.9. *Sforzando* or *fp* shape.

Staccato

This requires a quick attack and decay. This ensures that the note is short, but not dry.

FIGURE 3.10. Staccato shape.

FOUR

Attacks, Articulation, and Repeated Notes

IN CHAPTER 1, we learned a little about how to do a "soft attack"—by starting from nothing, blowing above the flute, and gradually lowering the airstream to gently let the note speak (without using the tongue). This is very useful for starting a soft melody, in the same way a singer would start an aria with a vowel, rather than a consonant ("Ave Maria," for example, shouldn't be "Tave Maria"!). Practice the *messa di voce* exercise (ex. 1.2) for soft attack.

Different Types of Attacks

In addition to the soft attack ("wa"), there are two other main types of attack: clear attack and hard attack. Clear attack can be without the tongue ("ha"), or with a soft tongue stroke, such as "da" or "ga" where the start of the note is immediate. "Peh" is useful to practice since it prepares the lips for soft, detached notes in the high register that need a clear beginning. However, "peh" starts from a position where the lips are closed, which stops the airstream, so rearticulating with "peh" will lead to gaps in between notes, which we want to avoid here. Hard attack is with the tongue, usually with consonants like "ka" and "ta," causing the start of the note to be very clearly pronounced. This is effective for strong, accented notes.

The following musical examples demonstrate the various types of attacks:

- Soft attack (without tongue—"wa"): Dutilleux. Sonatine (melody beginning on C♯) or Debussy. *Prélude à l'après-midi d'un faune* flute solo.

EXAMPLE 4.1. C. Debussy, *Prélude à l'après-midi d'un faune*, mm. 1–4.

- Clear attack (without tongue—"ha"): Debussy. *Syrinx* (opening).

EXAMPLE 4.2. C. Debussy, *Syrinx*, mm. 1–2.

- Clear attack with tongue ("da" or "ga"): Mozart. Concerto in G (first movement entry).

EXAMPLE 4.3. W. A. Mozart, Concerto in G Major K. 313, first movement, mm. 31–34.

- Hard attack ("ta" or "ka"): Ravel. *Chansons madécasses* (second movement—low articulated passage).

EXAMPLE 4.4. M. Ravel, "Aoua" from *Chansons madécasses*, mm. 38–41.

Here is an exercise to practice different attacks, which also helps with double tonguing. Soon, Saint-Saëns's "Volière" will seem a lot easier!

EXAMPLE 4.5. Exercise for practicing different attacks and double tonguing.

Articulation

The word *articulation* comes from the Latin *articulatio* which means joint or joining, for example, in anatomy, a hip joint. *Articulare* is the verb and to articulate means to form clear and distinct sounds in speech. Another example is an "articulated vehicle," where many sections are joined together by a pivoting joint. What we sometimes forget about articulation in music is this joining or connection. Many people will see articulated passages and immediately cut note lengths to make them sound "clear." This, however, is not always musical. Of course, there is music that requires very short note values that are separated by rests, but let us focus on a series of notes that do not have any slurs or staccato marks. Our aim is to make the notes clear, without losing the connection between them.

Try the following scale exercise, playing it tongued. Try to keep the notes connected by doing small bell tones on each. As in the previous chapter, as the notes get shorter, you simply need to do a quicker attack and decay. Remember to keep the pitch stable by adjusting with the lower lip or jaw. Try to do a small decay just towards the end of each note.

EXAMPLE 4.6. Scale exercise using bell tones.

Look at example 4.7 below, more commonly known as *Twinkle, Twinkle Little Star*.

EXAMPLE 4.7. W. A. Mozart, *Variations on* "Ah vous dirais-je, maman," K. 265, mm. 1–8, in *Variationen für das Pianoforte*.

Here we have one note per syllable, with repeated notes on each word. However, are those syllables joined together or detached? If you simply say the words "Twinkle, twinkle little star, How I wonder what you are," are the syllables connected? The answer is: yes. Try saying the same by making gaps between each syllable. Notice how this doesn't sound as "articulate" as the connected version. Therefore, by extension, we should learn to do the same on the flute. If we can achieve this, we can make the flute more expressive and closer in character to the voice.

Even when we are presented with staccato marks, we should question how long the composer wanted the note. Wibb often says, "Dot means long!" In other words, staccato markings don't always mean short. They can be a sign of expression. On other instruments, such as the piano, the note will continue to ring even if played short. The same is the case with a violin pizzicato. On the flute, we don't have the same resonating chamber as a violin or piano, and if we simply play the articulated notes short and dry, their melodic and expressive quality is lost.

EXAMPLE 4.8. F. Schubert, *Introduction and Variations on* "Trockne Blumen," op. 160, "Theme," mm. 9–12.

In the example above, staccatos are marked on the detached notes. To find a suitable length for these notes, we can study the text of the vocal score. See example 4.9 (notice that staccato markings are absent in the original).

EXAMPLE 4.9. F. Schubert, "Trockne Blumen" from *Die schöne Müllerin*, mm. 1–6 (vocal score) .

When you sing or say *"Ihr Blümlein alle, die sie mir gab, euch soll man legen mit mir ins Grab,"* you will notice that you do not cut or make gaps between the words or syllables. Additionally, listen to a recording of this work (such as that by Dietrich Fischer-Dieskau) and hear how the articulation is never short and dry. This is what you should aim for on the flute.

Repeated Notes

In order to achieve good repeated notes, we need to use what we learned with bell tones, but simply start with a T/D or K/G and make a connection between each note. When we tongue using the syllable "da" or "ga," we can prepare the tongue's position by placing it where we would say "nn," which can give a more rounded beginning to each note. This places the tongue just behind the teeth: "nnda" and "nnga."

Now say "dummm dummmm dummm" and notice that there is an initial attack on "dum" and then the sound continues through the "mmm," which connects to the next "dummm" without a gap.

DummmDummmDummm

FIGURE 4.1. Repeated notes.

So, to do this on the flute, we need to blow in a covered position while using the tip of our tongue to show a clear beginning (clear attack) and gradually uncover until such time that we need to rearticulate the note, not letting the note stop.

DO NOT:
- Stop the air supply before each note or breathe in between repeated notes.
- Cut each note with the tongue
- Play the second note louder

DO:
- Make the beginning of each note react to the consonant you pronounce and let it diminish so that the next note can start again clearly without having to be louder. We do not want unnecessary accents that affect the meter or stress.
- Pay attention to repeated notes. They come in different guises. Sometimes the repeated note arrives on a stronger beat from a weak beat (weak-strong), but it can also arrive on a weak beat from a strong beat (strong-weak). Look at the examples following:

Weak-strong

EXAMPLE 4.10. J. S. Bach, Sonata in E Major, BWV 1035, first movement, mm. 13–14.

Strong-weak

EXAMPLE 4.11. W. A. Mozart, *Variations on* "Ah vous dirais-je, maman," K. 265, mm. 1–8, in *Variationen für das Pianoforte.*

Remember, repeated notes need to be clear, but they still need to follow the grammar of the music. In other words, be careful where you place the stress. Avoid accenting the second beat of the bar in the above example since this will put the stress on a weak beat.

Play this repeated note exercise with a friend playing the melody from Elgar's *Chanson de matin.*

EXAMPLE 4.12. Repeated note exercise on Elgar's *Chanson de matin,* © Roderick Seed .

Another repeated note exercise is based on the opening theme from Vivaldi's "*La Notte*" concerto. Note the different lengths of notes for the repeated notes.

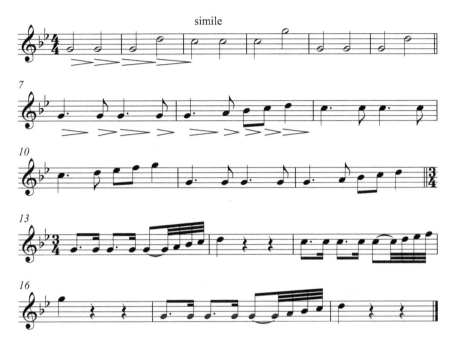

EXAMPLE 4.13. Bell tones and repeated notes exercise based on the first movement of A. Vivaldi, Concerto for Flute in G Minor, "La Notte." © Roderick Seed.

FIVE

Prosody: "Elephants and Taxis"

IN LINGUISTICS, PROSODY is the *rhythm, stress, and intonation of speech.*

Music written to words and poetry dates back to the Middle Ages (secular music of the troubadours and Gregorian chants set to religious texts), and composers used the natural rhythm, stress, and intonation of words in writing melodies. In terms of stress, composers can use different types of accents to reinforce the natural stress patterns of the text.

Different types of accents include:

1. Metric accents—placing the emphasis of a particular note on the strong beat of a bar.
2. Agogic accents—changing the lengths of notes to create emphasis.
3. Dynamic accents—emphasizing a syllable by playing or singing it louder
4. Melodic accents—using contour and melismatic effects.

We can therefore assume that composers had a natural sense of prosody when writing music. As performers, it is our obligation to understand and show this when we play. Singers have a natural advantage since they have the text, so instrumentalists need to find the text or the stress patterns in the score. Let us look at the stress patterns of certain words and how to show this with metric and dynamic accents.

Stress, Release, and Preparation

In language, words and phrases have parts which have a stress or emphasis. Other parts are released (no stress) or act as preparation for the stress.

Let's look at a few common words and phrases which William Bennett uses in his teaching:

TABLE 5.1. WHERE IS:

| the Stress (S)? | the Release (R)? | the Preparation (P)? |
S-R	S-R-R	P-S-R
ta-xi or *hap*-py	*el*-e-phant	I *love* you
dar-ling or *dear*-er	*pa*-ra-dise	ba-*na*-na

So, when we see figures in Mozart's music, like the one in the third bar of example 5.1, do we play: el-e-*phant* and accent the note D; or *el*-e-phant, with the stress on the first note A?

EXAMPLE 5.1. W. A. Mozart, Concerto no. 2 in D Major, K. 314, first movement, mm. 78–83.

We can find the answer in example 5.2. A similar figure in the second bar of this extract shows us how we should play:

al – – le - lu – ja, al - le - lu – ja,

EXAMPLE 5.2. W. A. Mozart, "Alleluia" from *Exsultate jubilate*, K. 165, mm. 37–40.

al-le-*lu*-ja = P-P-S-R

Naturally, we say *lu*—ja, not lu—*ja*. Likewise, *el*ephant not ele*phant*.

In addition, the articulation should not be cut short between "lu" and "ja." There is a natural connection between the syllables when spoken or sung. Therefore, we should aim to do that when we play it on the flute and try to find an articulation that connects the F♯ and the D in the Mozart concerto without a bump.

The "paradise" figure appears frequently in Mozart's music. Another example can be found in his famous piano sonata in C major. Notice how the harmony stays the same for the whole bar. It does not change on the second beat. Instead the phrase leads to the second bar where the harmony changes on the first beat of the bar, and where there is another "paradise," this time decorated with a trill on the "pa." This further explains why we should not accent the second beat. The concerto and alleluja examples above also follow the same harmonic pattern.

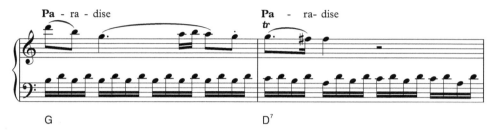

EXAMPLE 5.3. W. A. Mozart, Piano Sonata in C Major, K. 545, first movement, mm. 14–15.

"Paradise" Exercise

To practice this technique, have a look at the following exercise. Every three notes are an example of *pa*-ra-dise (*stress*-release-release). Show the repeated note and keep a connection between "ra" and "dise." One can use more vibrato on the first note of each group, which can help show the stress more clearly. Use less or no vibrato on the two released notes.

EXAMPLE 5.4. "Paradise" exercise (stress-release-release), © Roderick Seed.

Alleluja Vocalise

Then, practice this vocalise in multiple keys, remembering to take care of the second bar, so that the first beat is stronger than the second.

EXAMPLE 5.5. *Alleluja* vocalise, © Roderick Seed.

Mozart Concerto "Paradise" Vocalise

Finally, try the following vocalise on Mozart's Flute Concerto in D. Try playing it in multiple keys.

EXAMPLE 5.6. "Paradise" vocalise on W. A. Mozart, Concerto no. 2 in D Major, K. 314, © Roderick Seed.

An example of a "*ta*-xi" can be found in each of the first 4 bars of the next example by Handel.

EXAMPLE 5.7. G. F. Handel, Allegro from Flute Sonata in A Minor, HWV 374, mm. 1–8, in *Georg Friedrich Händels Werke.*

Like in the Mozart example, the harmony does not change on the second beat, so we should stress the first beat of the bar and play less for the second beat. Then we hear *ta*-xi, not ta-*xi*.

Here is an exercise to practice to this.

EXAMPLE 5.8. "Taxi" exercise, © Roderick Seed.

This brings us on to the topic of meter.

Meter

We've seen the influence of words on music. Another important factor for composers to consider comes from dance. This is especially important in Baroque partitas where each movement is a type of dance. Certain dances have certain time signatures or meters, where the **first beat of the bar should be stressed**. For example, for a Gigue in $\frac{6}{8}$, we feel 2 beats per bar, with the first stronger than the second. In a minuet or waltz, there is a clear emphasis on the first beat of three in each bar. When we play, we should try to show where the important beats are and therefore not stress the weak beats. The basic rule is to stress the first beat of the bar.

Be careful that a bar of $\frac{6}{8}$ does not sound the same as a bar of $\frac{3}{4}$.

EXAMPLE 5.9. Incorrect and correct stress.

We will look at how to practice meter in the next chapter using harmonics.

SIX

Harmonics Exercises

WE WILL NOW use harmonics to practice the technique of stress and release in more detail.

Always keep in mind the following shape:

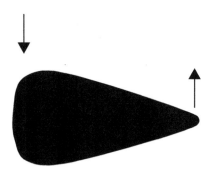

FIGURE 6.1. Cover and uncover .

For the first note (*forte)*, blow and cover, then gradually uncover. Lower lip back —> lower lip forward. It doesn't matter what register you are in, you still need to use the cover/uncover technique. Going from a higher note to a lower one, where there is a diminuendo, one still needs to lift the airstream. It is often tempting to cover more and aim the airstream down for lower notes to ensure that they sound, but this puts too much emphasis on them when it might not be desired in the music. These exercises work on breaking this habit.

In practicing the exercises, repeat the process for each bar, clearly showing the stress on the first beat. Use more vibrato on the stressed note and less for the weaker note. The exercise begins with two equal note lengths and then gets a bit harder when the rhythm changes.

The first exercise (ex. 6.1) is for practicing stress and release. Think of the word "dearer," where the stress is placed on "**dear**" and the "er" is released.

EXAMPLE 6.1.a. Stress and release exercise in $\frac{4}{4}$ ("dearer").

EXAMPLE 6.1.b. Stress and release exercise in $\frac{4}{4}$ ("dearer").

The next exercise is for preparation–stress (+ release). Uncover–cover–uncover.

Think about how you say these words: "prepare" and "believe." Both of these words begin with a preparation on the first syllable, and the second syllable is stressed: pre-*pare*, be-*lieve*. In $\frac{4}{4}$, the upbeat acts as the preparation.

EXAMPLE 6.2. Preparation, stress, and release exercise in $\frac{4}{4}$ ("believe").

The next exercise follows the same pattern, but this time in $\frac{3}{4}$.

EXAMPLE 6.3. Preparation, stress, and release exercise in $\frac{3}{4}$ ("believe").

Next, a stress and release exercise in $\frac{3}{4}$, starting from the downbeat, as in the word "*dear*-er."

EXAMPLE 6.4. Stress and release exercise in $\frac{3}{4}$ ("dearer").

Next, a similar exercise, but with a longer stressed note. Think of the word "*dar*-ling."

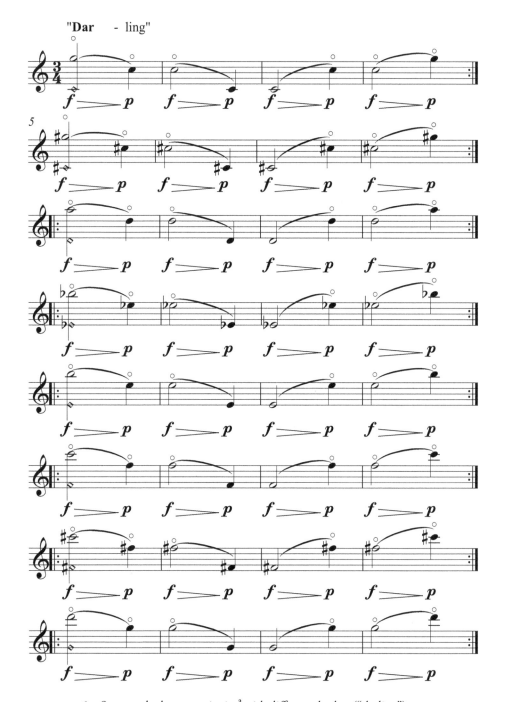

EXAMPLE 6.5. Stress and release exercise in ¾ with different rhythm ("darling").

The following exercise is a little harder, since it combines the technique for repeated notes with preparation, stress, and release. Think of the phrase "I *love* you," where the word "love" is stressed. ("I" is preparation and "you" is release.)

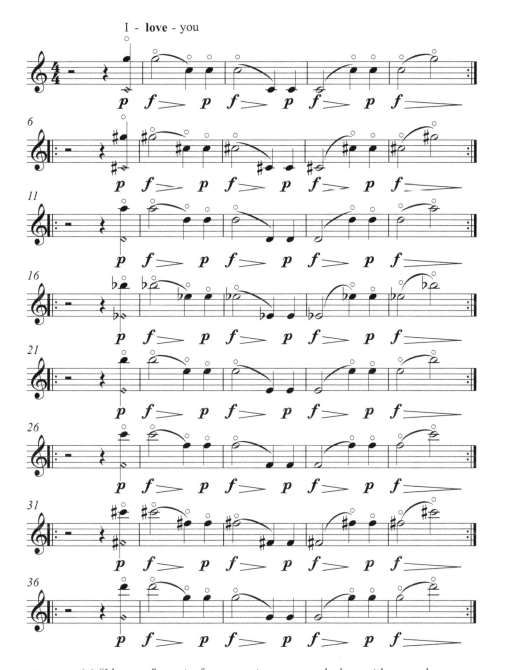

EXAMPLE 6.6. "I love you" exercise for preparation, stress, and release with repeated notes.

We can find a quicker example of "I *love* you" in the flute sonata by Martinu. Often, the stress is misplaced. For this example, the word potato ("po-*ta*-to") can be used since it is easier to say quickly. Notice in the bad example how the misplacement of the stress shifts the bar line, so that the pick-up notes become downbeats.

EXAMPLE 6.7. B. Martinu, First Sonata for Flute and Piano, third movement, mm. 75–78.

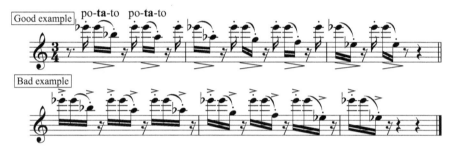

EXAMPLE 6.8. Correct and incorrect stress in the Martinu sonata.

When you do not diminish the last note of each group by blowing less and lifting the airstream (often because one wants to make sure of their low notes), we hear a stress on the last note and it misplaces the meter (see the *bad* example). Make sure that the pick-up notes are not louder than the first note of each slur. Remember, preparation–stress–release ("po-*ta*-to"). Practice the good example slowly, making sure to show the correct stress before increasing the tempo.

Look at example 6.9 below. Can you find "I [really] *love* you" and "*dar*-ling" in this piece of music? How many repeated notes are there? Are they weak-strong or strong-weak?

EXAMPLE 6.9. C. Saint-Saëns, *Romance*, op. 37, mm. 1–20.

Key RN: repeated notes.

Putting Words to Melodies

EXAMPLE 6.10. P. Tchaikovsky, Andante cantabile from Symphony no. 5, op. 64, mm. 1–12 (horn solo).

You can try putting words to melodies like the one above. They don't need to be the most profound words ever written. For example, for the above melody, we could use the words:

"I am so *hun*gry, terribly *hun*gry, I did not eat lunch today—how *aw*ful!"

Notice how the phrase markings follow the natural stress and release of the words.

Finding the Skeleton

EXAMPLE 6.11. Practicing the skeleton of H. Purcell, Air in D Minor, © Roderick Seed.

When approaching a melody like Purcell's Air, we can practice the "skeleton" or outline of the melody as seen above. By practicing the attack and decay only on the first note of each bar, we are practicing the movement required by our lips for the whole bar when further notes are added. We want to make sure that the first beat has more stress than the second or third. So, when we add notes to the skeleton, try to blow the same as you did when it was just one note to a bar, thereby not accenting the weaker beats.

The next step is to show the bigger phrase. I like to think of this as "microphrasing" and "macrophrasing," where the microphrasing is making a beautiful shape within a bar and macrophrasing is making a beautiful shape *within the whole phrase*. Therefore, one needs to make a decision as to where your phrase is going and not make each bar have the same stress or dynamic. There needs to be a direction.

The same applies with language: every word has its own stress and release, but some words have more importance than others in a phrase. Indeed, emphasizing different words can change the meaning:

- **I'm** not playing the flute today (*Sheila* is)
- I'm **not** playing the flute today (Someone thought I was)
- I'm not **playing** the flute today (I'm *fixing* it)
- I'm not playing the **flute** today (I'm playing the *piano*)
- I'm not playing the flute **today** (It's my day off)

Notice how the meaning changes when you highlight different words in the sentence. So, in musical phrasing, we need to find out which part of the phrase is the most important and phrase accordingly.

SEVEN

Shakuhachi Exercise for Embouchure Control

THIS IS AN exercise that I learned in the William Bennett Flute Summer School when I was younger. It can take a while to master, but it is well worth it. By trying to find a sound using just the body of the flute, we can practice finding a good tone without undue pressure. The focus of this exercise is to find a good angle for blowing the air so that it is directed to the area that gives the greatest resonance.

Start by blowing forward and bring the body of the flute (not the headjoint!) vertically toward you. Feel the edge under your lower lip and experiment with the angle at which the flute faces you. Try a covered position and slowly move to a less covered position. Make sure air is not escaping at the front edge. Finger a C2 and work on getting a focused tone. Then try moving down chromatically to G1.

This exercise is particularly useful for notes in the low register. By releasing tension in the corners of the lips, one can find a sound which is less restricted and more flexible. Notice from the picture the shape of the lips.

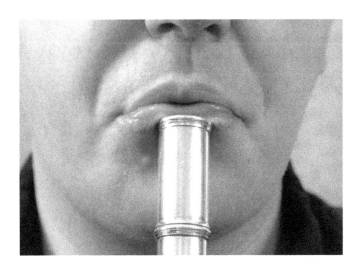

FIGURE 7.1. The shakuhachi exercise using just the body joint of the flute.

Now think about your embouchure. Is it too tight? Is it too relaxed? Where is the airstream directed? Are you aiming for the far edge? How much air do you need?

Once I have found the sound, I like to play the following, which sounds similar to the melody from Debussy's "*La fille aux cheveux de lin*" (Girl with the Flaxen Hair).

EXAMPLE 7.1. Shakuhachi vocalise on a theme by C. Debussy.

EIGHT

Intonation Exercises

WE HAVE LOOKED at how to change the pitch and how to adjust when we are flat and sharp, but we have not yet looked at intervals. A good exercise for practicing intervals actually comes from the opening bars of the Introduction to Schubert's *Introduction and Variations on* "Trockne Blumen" (ex. 8.2 below). This opening is very exposed and can often sound flat even after tuning with the piano. Why?

Equal Temperament

Keyboard instruments are tuned using equal temperament, a compromised tuning system, so that we can play with uniform intonation in any key. The system made all semitones equal (exactly half a standard tone) and it allowed composers to modulate on an instrument with fixed pitches. However, compared to the harmonic series (or the "just scale"), intervals played on the keyboard are not quite in tune and therefore do not produce a pleasing sound. If you practice intervals with a friend or with a tuning machine, you can listen for another sound, which we call the "difference tone." This occurs when the frequency of the lower note is subtracted from the frequency of the higher note, leaving another note sounding. For example, with an octave: $A_2 = 880\text{Hz}$ minus $A_1 = 440\text{Hz} = 440\text{Hz}$ (A). When this is in tune, we hear a pleasing, ringing sound. If the higher A is too sharp (881Hz), we get a difference tone that is too sharp (441Hz), which clashes with the lower A (440Hz). Likewise, if the higher A is too flat, we the difference tone will also be flat and clash with the lower A. When this happens, we hear a pulsation or "beats," where the frequencies are not vibrating at the same rate. This principle also applies to the harmonics in one note (*harmonics in tune*). If the harmonics are in tune, then we hear a full resonant sound and the sound projects with ease.

TABLE 8.1. RELATIONSHIP BETWEEN THE JUST SCALE AND EQUAL TEMPERAMENT, AND THE ADJUSTMENT REQUIRED WHEN PLAYING THE UPPER NOTE OF A TWO-NOTE INTERVAL

Interval	Ratio to Fundamental *Just Scale*	Ratio to Fundamental *Equal Temperament*	Adjustment required to get upper note in tune
Unison	1.0000	1.00000	—
Minor 2nd	25/24 = 1.0417	1.05946	↓
Major 2nd	9/8 = 1.1250	1.12246	↑
Minor 3rd	6/5 = 1.2000	1.18921	↑
Major 3rd	5/4 = 1.2500	1.25992	↓
Perfect 4th	4/3 = 1.3333	1.33483	↓
Diminished 5th	45/32 = 1.4063	1.41421	↓
Perfect 5th	3/2 = 1.5000	1.49831	↑
Minor 6th	8/5 = 1.6000	1.58740	↑
Major 6th	5/3 = 1.6667	1.68179	↓
Minor 7th	9/5 = 1.8000	1.78180	↑
Major 7th	15/8 = 1.8750	1.88775	↓
Octave	2.0000	2.00000	—

In table 8.1, we can see what adjustments we need to do when we are playing intervals above another instrument. If we simply play a note that is in tune according to the tuning machine, we will not get a true, satisfying interval, since the difference tone will be out of place.

Finding the Difference Tone

Here is an exercise to practice finding the difference tone.

Practice this with a friend or teacher, or with your tuning machine or keyboard. Don't move onto the next note until you can clearly hear the difference tone and that it's in the right place. Make sure your difference tone is in tune! Try pitch bending and notice how the difference tone changes.

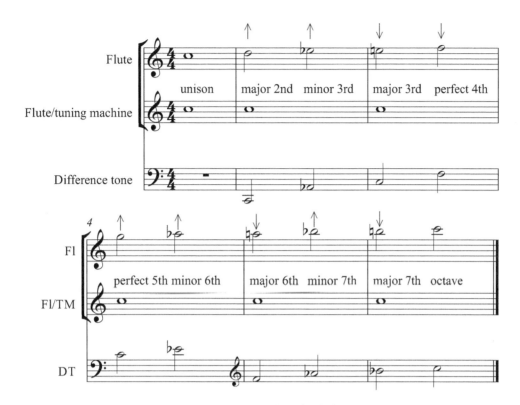

EXAMPLE 8.1. Intonation exercise: Finding the difference tone.

Key ↑ = raise the pitch ↓ = lower the pitch

Schubert Intonation Exercise

Practice the exercises below in any key, slowly. Play the top line of each exercise. It is best to practice this quietly, so you can really listen to your intonation. If using the sound from the tuning machine, use the second example and just leave it as a pedal. The first example uses the actual bass line that Schubert wrote. Can you hear the difference tones? Try changing the pitch and notice how the difference tone moves in the opposite direction!

EXAMPLE 8.2. Intonation exercise based on the opening of F. Schubert, "Trockne Blumen" variations—with piano.

EXAMPLE 8.3. Intonation exercise based on the opening of F. Schubert, "Trockne Blumen" variations—with a tuning machine.

Key ↑ = raise the pitch ↓ = lower the pitch

So, as you can see, playing the Introduction from Schubert's "Trockne Blumen" is quite difficult, but this is a good way to practice it.

Practicing intonation in this way is particularly useful for orchestral playing. For example, you might have a passage in major thirds with another flute player, so both of you can adjust the pitch to make the interval sound pleasing, where the upper part can be played slightly flatter, and the lower part can be played slightly sharper. This shares the burden of adjusting the pitch. Alternatively, you might be playing a chord in the woodwind section where you have the perfect 5th, so you need to make sure it is pitched high enough to make it a true perfect 5th.

Scales with Good Intonation

When you practice Taffanel & Gaubert scales, try to think about the intervals you are playing. For example, in the scale sequence below, you want to make sure the 5th is sharp enough, so follow the notes with your lips. The same applies for the 9th, which is the dominant of the dominant, or a compound major 2nd. It also needs to be raised.

For the diminished 5th, this needs to be slightly lower in pitch.

EXAMPLE 8.4. Scales with good intonation based on Taffanel & Gaubert, *Exercises journaliers*, in *Méthode complète de flûte*.

Key ↑ = Raise the perfect 5th (and 9th) degree of the scale
↓ = lower the diminished 5th

Alternative Fingerings to Help with Intonation

Sharp ("Sensitive") Fingerings

These will help with quiet notes that tend to be flat. You will not need to adjust too much with the embouchure for these notes, so the tone does not lose focus. You can try finding your own fingerings if these do not work well on your flute. Sensitive fingerings also offer an alternative color, which can be very effective.

B♭3

EXAMPLE 8.5. G. Bizet, "Entr'acte" from *Carmen*, mm. 7–11.

D3 natural

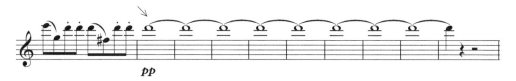

EXAMPLE 8.6. L. van Beethoven, *Leonore Overture no.3*, op. 72b, mm. 351–60.

D♭3

EXAMPLE 8.7. F. Poulenc, Sonata for Flute and Piano, second movement, mm. 60–61 .

C3 natural

EXAMPLE 8.8. C. M. Widor, "Romance" from Suite, op. 34, mm. 87–91.

B2 natural (or B3 natural if you have a flute with a B footjoint)

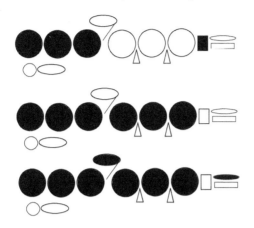

EXAMPLE 8.9. C. Reinecke, Concerto, op. 283, second movement, mm. 70–72.

EXAMPLE 8.10. F. Mendelssohn, *Hebrides Overture*, mm. 262–268.

B♭2

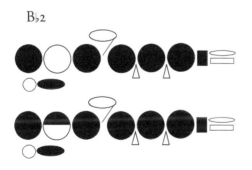

EXAMPLE 8.11. C. Debussy, *Syrinx*, mm. 6–8.

EXAMPLE 8.12. P. Gaubert, *Nocturne et allegro scherzando,* mm. 33–34.

A2 natural

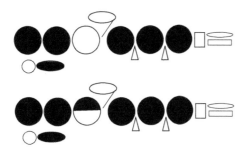

EXAMPLE 8.13. C. Franck, Violin Sonata in A Major, first movement, mm. 115–17.

A♭2

EXAMPLE 8.14. C. Saint-Saëns, *Romance,* op. 37, mm. 87–95.

D♭2

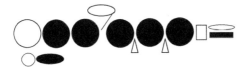

EXAMPLE 8.15. C. Debussy, *Syrinx*, mm. 16–17.

C2 natural

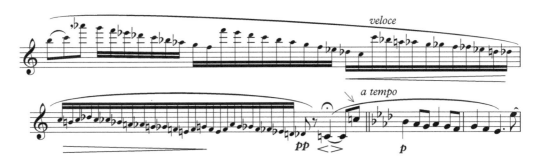

EXAMPLE 8.16. C. M. Widor, "Romance" from Suite, op. 34, mm. 62–65.

Flat Fingerings

These fingerings will help in loud dynamics if the notes are too sharp or bright without the player having to cover the mouth hole so much with the lower lip, thereby producing a fuller tone.

E♭3

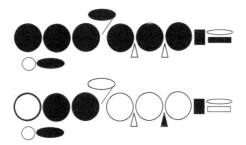

E3 natural (no E♭ key)

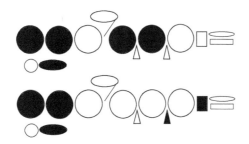

F3 natural

F♯3

G♯3

For an even flatter G♯, take off the E♭ key.

A3 natural

G3 natural

You can try the standard fingerings for F3 natural or F♯3 without the thumb. The quality of sound is not terribly pleasant, but it can be useful in situations where you need to play very loudly in the orchestra but don't want to be sharper than everybody else!

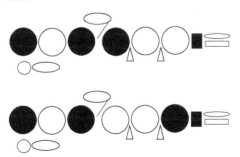

NINE

Flexibility Exercises

Godard Vocalise

EXAMPLE 9.1.a. Flexibility exercise based on Godard, Allegretto

2

EXAMPLE 9.1.b. Flexibility exercise based on Godard, Allegretto

The above exercise is based upon Godard's Allegretto. Its skeleton is a dominant 7th, with a sequential pattern of one note followed by another a semitone lower, then another a whole tone higher, finally returning to the original note. It is important to make especially sure that the higher note is softer than the first note, that is, don't blow more for the higher note. Instead, lift the airstream (uncover) to ensure it is not flat.

Practice in all dynamics.

Inverted Headjoint Exercise for Lifting the Airstream

With the flute fully assembled, turn the headjoint around so that the lip plate is facing the ground while you hold the flute normally. Now place the flute above your top lip and blow *upward* so that the air is still hitting the outer edge. This is a good exercise for lower lip flexibility—especially for playing sharper in quiet dynamics so that the pitch does not fall flat. Try playing scales or long tone exercises with the headjoint inverted like this.

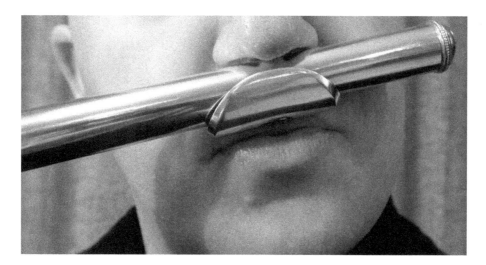

FIGURE 9.1. Inverted headjoint exercise.

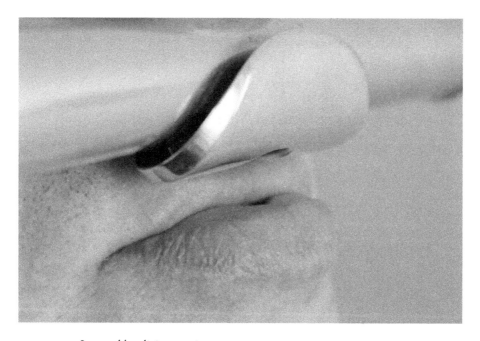

FIGURE 9.2. Inverted headjoint exercise.

TEN

Other Exercises: Whistle Tones and Vocalizes

"Rigamazaar" Vocalize

Here is a vocalize called "Rigamazaar" (a made-up word) that Wibb uses to practice finding a brilliant, vibrant sound. Phrase towards each "zaar" and make sure those notes have a good, ringing sound. Each "Ri-ga-ma" act as a preparation to "zaar" and should be quick, except for the last one, where you should find a hollower color (known as *détimbré*) and which should be played more slowly than the preceding *timbré* figures. Sing it first then practice in all keys.

Whistle Tones

When I studied with Wibb, he would often warm up with a few whistle tones. I asked him why he did this and he showed me that by practicing whistle tones, one can get the lips in a good shape for blowing. Whistle tones also help relax the lips if they feel tight. He referred to it as "target practice," making one more aware of the size of the jet of air and where it enters the flute. It encourages a steady airstream that will help produce a stable sound. If you can get a whistle tone that doesn't jump around the harmonic series, your sound will be more stable.

To get a good whistle tone, one needs to form a round shape with the lips (as if whistling) and blow very gently across the mouth hole, but with a fairly fast air speed. One way of obtaining a good whistle tone is to play, for example, a low G (G1) and do a diminuendo with relaxed lips. From there, try to move up to the next harmonic (G2). You will most likely get a whistle tone of one of the upper harmonics instead of the actual G2 note you were aiming for.

EXAMPLE 10.1. "*Rigamazaar*" exercise for a vibrant sound.

The challenge with whistle tones is to keep the tone constant. Try moving up and down the harmonic series in a controlled fashion, isolating each harmonic. For the lower whistle tones, one needs to blow with a slightly slower and rounder jet of air aimed lower in the chimney of the flute.

EXAMPLE 10.2. Whistle tone exercise as harmonics of low C .

You can also practice specific pitches using whistle tones by fingering notes in the high register. I have taken the opening of Schubert's Introduction and Variations and put it two octaves higher and transposed it into other keys. You can do this with any melody.

EXAMPLE 10.3. Whistle tone exercise based on the opening of F. Schubert, "Trockne Blumen," © Roderick Seed.

Exercise Based on "Somewhere Over the Rainbow"

The next tone exercise uses the melody from "Somewhere Over the Rainbow." Notice how the phrase leads to the second bar. Continue this phrasing in exercises (a) and (b), so that the octave leap does not disrupt the musical line. Use your best sound from the low note and transfer that to the next bar. Remember to finish the note beautifully and in tune!

EXAMPLE 10.4. "Somewhere Over the Rainbow" exercises (a) and (b), © Roderick Seed.

Exercise on Godard's "Idylle"

EXAMPLE 10.5. B. Godard, "Idylle," mm. 27–30.

The following exercise based on the Godard "Idylle" combines the technique for playing repeated notes, getting reaction in the sound, and *messa di voce* (see ex. 1.2). Repeat this exercise an octave higher.

EXAMPLE 10.6. Exercise based on Godard, "Idylle," © Roderick Seed.

Middle E and F Exercises

Unlike middle E♭ or D natural, middle E is fingered exactly the same as its lower octave relative. E♭ and D natural have the advantage of venting the first tone hole, which makes it easier for the second octave to speak cleanly. We should therefore practice finding exactly where middle E is in comparison to the other harmonics.

EXAMPLE 10.7. Using harmonics to find middle E.

Use Harmonics to Find Middle E

Middle E lies between the fundamental low E and its third harmonic—B natural. Finger a low E and use your lips to change the speed and direction of the air to alternate between the low E and the harmonic as shown in the first bar, without getting louder. Once you are comfortable doing that, move onto the second bar. The middle E will need a slightly slower air speed than the B natural harmonic, but not as slow as the low E (the air speed of middle E is twice as fast as low E). The angle at which you direct the airstream will be slightly lower than the harmonic, but higher than the low E. Once you have found it, hold it. Then repeat the exercise.

"Cheat Fingering"

You may be familiar with the fingering for E2 below:

Instead of using your right-hand little finger on just the E♭ key, you press both the E♭ key and the C♯ key.

Look at the figure below. With the standard fingering, we can play all the harmonics up to high G♯ (the fifth harmonic) with relative ease. Top B is very difficult to get, although it is the next note in the series. With the cheat middle E fingering, the fifth harmonic (G♯) is bypassed, so that you either get E3 or top B (B3). The addition of the C♯ key facilitates the production of the top B harmonic. Top B is also the seventh harmonic in the series for low C♯ (C♯1). The enhanced presence of these harmonics improves the clarity of the middle E.

This is particularly useful in passages with repeated Es. For example, Piazzolla's "Night Club 1960" from *Histoire du Tango*.

Interestingly, this works the exact same way for F♯2. Simply add the C♯ key to the standard fingering.

EXAMPLE 10.8. Harmonics of E produced with different fingerings.

The cheat fingering for F2 natural is the same as the standard fingering, just minus the E♭ key, which affects the harmonics in the same way as it does for middle E.

F2 natural

EXAMPLE 10.9. Harmonic series for F on the flute with different fingerings.

Taffanel & Gaubert Scales

EXAMPLE 10.10. Scale exercise for middle E based on Taffanel & Gaubert,
Exercises journaliers, no.1, in *Méthode complète de flûte*.

In the example based on *Exercises journaliers* no.1, as Wibb would say, "Follow the
notes with your lips," so that when you reach E, the air direction is higher. Keep the
embouchure round, as in the vowel shape "oo."

ELEVEN

Approaching Melodies

IN ADDITION TO preparing: an etude by Andersen, for example, a study or two from the Moyse *24 Studies*, Taffanel & Gaubert scales, and repertoire, I would also bring a melody (usually from *Tone Development through Interpretation* by Moyse) to my lessons with Wibb. Here is an example of a melody we studied:

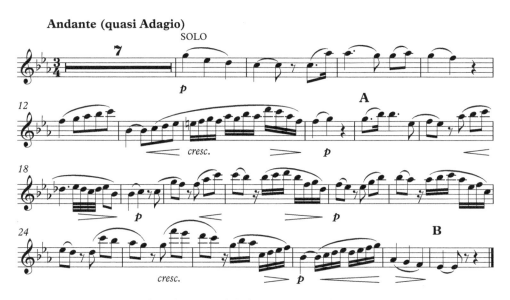

EXAMPLE 11.1. C. Gounod, Andante cantabile from *Petite Symphonie*, mm. 1–29.

This beautiful melody is great for practicing all the topics discussed in this book and is useful as a good summary. Here are a few points to consider:

Appoggiaturas

Show good stress and release, for example, in bars 11, 15, 17, 19, 20, 21, 22, 23, 24, 25, 26. Think of the word "darling" to help you give the correct stress.

Meter

Show the meter correctly—this piece is in $\frac{3}{4}$ not $\frac{6}{8}$. The first beat should be stronger than second and third, and the eighth notes (quavers) should be grouped in three groups of two, rather than two groups of three.

Repeated Notes

In this example, the repeated notes come from a weak beat and are repeated on a strong beat. Make sure they are clear without unnecessary gaps or heavy accents.

Questions to Ask Yourself

- How long are the phrases? Where do the phrases go?
- What is the character? What color is suitable? Use the harmonies to help form your choice of color and character.
- What are the words? Think of some words which match the stress and rhythm of the music.

Soft Attack

The beginning shouldn't start with a strong consonant attack but more of a vowel, like "ah." Practice on the third harmonic of low C with soft attack. The upbeats also need to be taken care of so they act as preparation for the downbeat. In other words, do not accent the beginning of the upbeat eighth notes.

Intonation

Be especially careful of the D♭ in bar 18—be prepared to cover more for this note. A lot of flutes have misplaced D♭/C♯ tone holes, which affect color and intonation.

Legato Intervals

Use the lips and support the airstream so that large intervals do not disrupt the meter or shape of the phrase, and the legato line remains smooth, in, for example, the leap in bar 25.

Expressive Tone

Use different vibrato speeds and depths depending on the harmony and the phrasing. For example, as the phrase becomes more intense, use a more intense vibrato.

Tone Color

Use different tone colors to highlight the different keys. At the beginning, it is major, but when the harmony changes in bar 20, use a softer color.

Transpose and Memorize

After looking at all the above, I would then play the example in about three different keys (a semitone higher or lower, a minor 3rd or major 3rd higher, for example). Make sure you change the key signature when transposing.

All the transposed melodies should be played from memory. By memorizing, you can familiarize yourself with all the intervals, free yourself from the music stand, and listen carefully to what you are playing. For example, ask yourself: Was the intonation good? Did I do a good soft attack? Is my vibrato suitable for this part of the melody?

Bibliography

Alcantara, Pedro De. *Integrated Practice: Coordination, Rhythm & Sound*. New York: Oxford University Press, 2011.

Bach, Johann Sebastian. Partita in A Minor for Flute Alone, BWV 1013. Edited by Hans-Peter Schmitz. Kassel: Bärenreiter, 1963.

Bach, Johann Sebastian. Sonata in E Major, BWV 1035. Edited by William Bennett. London: Chester Music, 1983.

Beethoven, Ludwig van. *Leonore Overture no.3,* op. 72b. Leipzig: Breitkopf & Härtel, 1862.

Bizet, Georges. "Entr'acte" from *Carmen*. Accessed July 8, 2015. http://www.flutetunes.com /tunes.php?id=171.

Debussy, Claude. *La fille aux cheveux de lin*. Paris: Durand, 1910.

Debussy, Claude. *Prélude à l'après-midi d'un faune*. New York: Edwin F. Kalmus, c. 1951.

Debussy, Claude. *Syrinx*. For solo flute. Paris: Jobert, 1927.

Elgar, Edward. *Chanson de matin*. London: Novello, 1897.

Enesco, Georges. *Cantabile et Presto*. Paris: Enoch, c. 1904.

Franck, César. Sonata for Violin and Piano. Edited by Leopold Lichtenburg and Clarence Adler. New York: G. Schirmer, 1915.

Gaubert, Philippe. *Nocturne et allegro scherzando*. Paris: Enoch, 1906.

Godard, Benjamin. "Idylle" from *Suite de trois morceaux*, op.116. Paris: Durand et Schœnewerk, c. 1889.

Gounod, Charles. *Petite Symphonie*. Paris: Costallat, 1904.

Handel, George Frederic. *Georg Friedrich Händels Werke*. Edited by Friedrich W. Chrysander. Leipzig: Deutsche Händelgesellschaft, 1879.

Johnston, Ian. *Measured Tones: The Interplay of Physics and Music*. Bristol: Institute of Physics, 2002.

Karg-Elert, Sigfrid. *30 Caprices for Flute*, op. 107. Leipzig: Steingräber Verlag, 1918.

Martinu, Bohuslav. First Sonata for Flute and Piano. New York: Associated Music Publishers, 1951.

Mendelssohn, Felix. *Hebrides Overture*, op.26. Leipzig: Breitkopf & Härtel, c.1890.

Moyse, Marcel. *De la sonorite: Art et technique*. Paris: A. Leduc, 1934.

Moyse, Marcel. Tone Development through Interpretation for the Flute. McGinnis & Marx, 1986.

Moyse, Marcel. *Vingt-quatre petites études mélodiques avec variations*. Paris: A. Leduc, 1932.

Mozart, Wolfgang Amadeus. Concerto in G Major, K. 313. Arranged by August Horn. Leipzig: Breitkopf & Härtel, c. 1894.

Mozart, Wolfgang Amadeus. *Exsultate, Jubilate*, KV 165 (158a). Edited by Paul Klengel. Durchgesehene Neuaufl. ed. Wiesbaden: Breitkopf & Härtel, 1986.

Mozart, Wolfgang Amadeus. Flute Concerto no.2 in D Major, K. 314. Arranged by Carl Burchard. Leipzig: Breitkopf & Härtel, 1924.

Mozart, Wolfgang Amadeus. Piano Sonata in C Major, K. 545. Leipzig: Breitkopf & Härtel, 1878.

Mozart, Wolfgang Amadeus. *Variationen für das Pianoforte*, no.6. Leipzig: Breitkopf & Härtel, 1878.

Poulenc, Francis. Sonata for Flute and Piano. London: J. & W. Chester, 1958.

Purcell, Henry. Air in D Minor, ZT 676. Accessed July 8, 2015. https://www.flutetunes.com/tunes.php?id=436

Ravel, Maurice. *Chansons madécasses*. Paris: Durand, 1926.

Reinecke, Carl. Flute Concerto, op.283. Leipzig: Breitkopf & Härtel, 1909.

Saint-Saëns, Camille. *Romance*, op. 37. Paris: Durand et Schoenewerk, 1953.

Schubert, Franz. *Introduction and Variations on* "Trockne Blumen," D. 802. Leipzig: Breitkopf & Härtel, 1886.

Schubert, Franz. "Trockne Blumen" from *Die schöne Müllerin*. In *Gesänge für eine Singstimme mit Klavierbegleitung*. Leipzig: C. F. Peters, 1928.

Suits, B. H. Physics of Music—Notes: Scales: Just vs Equal Temperament. Physics Department, Michigan Technological University. http://www.phy.mtu.edu/~suits/scales.html.

Taffanel, Claude Paul, and Philippe Gaubert. *Méthode complète de flûte*. Nouv. ed. Paris: A. Leduc, 1958.

Tchaikovsky, Pyotr Il'yich. Symphony no. 5, op. 64. Arranged for piano four hands by Sergey Taneyev. Moscow: Jurgenson.

Vivaldi, Antonio. Concerto for Flute in G Minor, RV. 439, "La Notte." Milan: Ricordi, 1982.

Widor, Charles-Marie. Suite, op. 34. Paris: Heugel.

Index

Page numbers in italics refer to figures. Entries for musical works lead to excerpts or adaptations to illustrate technique.

WILLIAM BENNETT teaches at the Royal Academy of Music in London and is one of the foremost musical artists performing today. He has raised the profile of the flute to that of an instrument capable of a wide range of tonal colors, dynamics, and expression, giving it the depth, dignity, and grandeur of the voice or a string instrument. Bennett has been principal flute in many orchestras, including the London Symphony, the Academy of St. Martin in the Fields, and the English Chamber Orchestra, and has recorded over three hundred works for flute. Bennett gives master classes all over the world and the Queen has presented Bennett with the Most Excellent Order of the British Empire (OBE) for his distinguished Services to Music.

RODERICK SEED is a British flute player based in Vancouver, BC, who made his Carnegie Hall debut in 2010 after winning First Prize at the Alexander and Buono International Flute Competition. He is a graduate of the Royal Academy of Music, London, where he won an entrance scholarship to study with William Bennett, Kate Hill, and Patricia Morris. Seed has performed and taught internationally. Currently he teaches at the Vancouver Symphony Orchestra School of Music and performs with the Vancouver Symphony Orchestra.

CPSIA information can be obtained
at www.ICGtesting.com
Printed in the USA
BVHW022057280422
635619BV00025B/382